CAKERY
CROCHET

**9 Colorful Projects
Using Yarn Cakes**

LEISURE ARTS, INC. • Maumelle, Arkansas

Contents

LION BRAND® FERRIS WHEEL

Abigail Mitts

 **EASY**

SIZES

Finished Circumference:
About 9 in. (23 cm)

Finished Length:
About 9 in. (23 cm)

GAUGE

6 V-sts = about 4 in. (10 cm).

BE SURE TO CHECK YOUR GAUGE.

MATERIALS

Yarn (Medium) **4**
  Lion Brand® FERRIS WHEEL
  (Art. #217)

☐ #605 Buttercup 1 cake

☐ Lion Brand® crochet hook
  size H-8 (5 mm)

☐ Lion Brand® large-eyed
  blunt needle

NOTES

1. Mitts are working in joined rnds, with RS always facing.
   Do not turn at beginning of rnds unless otherwise indicated.

2. The thumb opening is worked back and forth in rows.

STITCH EXPLANATION

V-st (V-stitch) Work 2 dc in indicated st or sp.

MITTS *(Make 2)*

Ch 28, join with a sl st in first ch to make a ring.

Rnd 1: Ch 3 (counts as dc), *sk next ch, V-st in next ch; rep from * to last ch, sk last ch; join with sl st in top of beg ch-3 – you will have 13 V-sts and 1 dc in this rnd.

Rnds 2-10: Ch 3 (counts as dc), V-st in sp between dc sts of each V-st around; join with sl st in top of beg ch-3.

Thumb Opening

Rows 11-14: Ch 3, TURN, V-st in sp between dc sts of each V-st across, dc in top of beg ch-3 – 13 V-sts and 2 dc.

Sl st in top of beg ch-3 of last rnd to continue working in rnds.

Rnds 15-18: Ch 3, do NOT turn, V-st in sp between dc sts of each V-st around, join with sl st in beg ch-3.

Fasten off.

FINISHING

Weave in ends.

LION BRAND® MANDALA® SPARKLE

Elle Shawl

 **EASY**

SIZE

About 26 x 52 in. (66 x 132 cm) at longest and widest points

GAUGE

8 sts [two (3 dc, ch 1) groups] = about 3½ in. (9 cm); 7 rows = about 4½ in. (11.5 cm).

BE SURE TO CHECK YOUR GAUGE.

MATERIALS

Yarn (Light)

Lion Brand® MANDALA® SPARKLE (Art. #527)

☐ #315 Aquarius 2 cakes

☐ Lion Brand® crochet hook size H-8 (5 mm)

☐ Lion Brand® large-eyed blunt needle

NOTES

1. Shawl is worked in one piece, back and forth in rows, beginning at center of top edge.

2. Increases are worked to shape the Shawl.

3. A final edging rnd is worked all the way around outer edges of Shawl.

4. For those who find a visual helpful, we've included a stitch diagram.

SHAWL

Ch 5.

Row 1 (RS): (3 Dc, ch 2, 3 dc, ch 1, dc) in 5th ch from hook (4 skipped ch count as dc, ch 1) – you will have two 3-dc groups in this row.

Row 2: Ch 4 (counts as dc, ch 1), turn, 3 dc in first ch-1 sp, ch 1, (3 dc, ch 2, 3 dc) in next ch-2 sp, ch 1, 3 dc in beg ch-sp, ch 1, dc in 3rd ch of beg ch – Four 3-dc groups.

Row 3: Ch 4 (counts as dc, ch 1), turn, 3 dc in first ch-1 sp, ch 1, 3 dc in next ch-1 sp, ch 1, (3 dc, ch 2, 3 dc) in next ch-2 sp, ch 1, 3 dc in next ch-1 sp, ch 1, 3 dc in beg ch-sp, ch 1, dc in 3rd ch of beg ch-4 – Six 3-dc groups.

Row 4: Ch 4 (counts as dc, ch 1), turn, 3 dc in first ch-1 sp, (ch 1, 3 dc in next ch-1 sp) 2 times, ch 1, (3 dc, ch 2, 3 dc) in next ch-2 sp, (ch 1, 3 dc in next ch-1 sp) 2 times, ch 1, 3 dc in beg ch-sp, ch 1, dc in 3rd ch of beg ch-4 – Eight 3-dc groups.

Rows 5-38: Ch 4 (counts as dc, ch 1), turn, 3 dc in first ch-1 sp, *ch 1, 3 dc in next ch-1 sp; rep from * to center ch-2 sp, ch 1, (3 dc, ch 2, 3 dc) in center ch-2 sp, **ch 1, 3 dc in next ch-1 sp; rep from ** to beg ch-sp, ch 1, 3 dc in beg ch-sp, ch 1, dc in 3rd ch of beg ch-4 – Seventy-six 3-dc groups in Row 38.

Row 39: Ch 3 (counts as hdc, ch 1), turn, hdc in first ch-1 sp, hdc in each st and ch-1 sp to center ch-2 sp, (2 hdc, ch 2, 2 hdc) in center ch-2 sp, hdc in each st and ch-1 sp to beg ch-sp, hdc in beg ch-sp, ch 1, hdc in 3rd ch of beg ch-4 – 310 hdc, 2 ch-1 sps, and 1 center ch-2 sp.

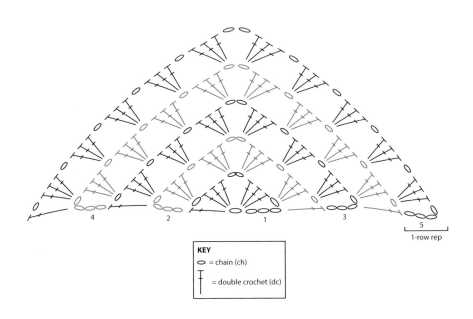

4 2 1 3

5
1-row rep

KEY
⌒ = chain (ch)
† = double crochet (dc)

Row 40: Ch 3 (counts as hdc, ch 1), turn, hdc in first ch-1 sp, hdc in each hdc to center ch-2 sp, (2 hdc, ch 2, 2 hdc) in center ch-2 sp, hdc in each st to beg ch-sp, hdc in beg ch-sp, ch 1, hdc in 2nd ch of beg ch-3 – 316 hdc, 2 ch-1 sps, and 1 center ch-2 sp.

Edging Rnd
Ch 3 (counts as hdc, ch 1), turn, hdc in first ch-1 sp, hdc in each hdc to center ch-2 sp, 4 hdc in center ch-2 sp, hdc in each hdc to beg ch-sp, hdc in beg ch-sp, ch 1, hdc in 2nd ch of beg ch-3; working in ends of rows along top edge, work hdc evenly spaced along top edge; join with slip st in 2nd ch of beg ch-3.

Fasten off.

FINISHING
Weave in ends.

Bianca Top

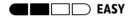 **EASY**

SIZES

S/M (L/1X)

Finished Bust:
About 42 (50) in.
[106.5 (127) cm]

Finished Length:
About 24 (25) in. [61 (63.5) cm]

Note: Pattern is written for
smaller size with changes for
larger size in parentheses.
When only one number is given,
it applies to both sizes. To follow
pattern more easily, circle all
numbers pertaining to your
size before beginning.

GAUGE

16 dc + 9 rows = about 4 in.
(10 cm).

BE SURE TO CHECK YOUR GAUGE.

MATERIALS

Yarn (Medium) **4**
LION BRAND® SHAWL
IN A CAKE (Art. #455)

☐ #305 Wind Chimes
3 (4) cakes

☐ Lion Brand® crochet hook
size H-8 (5 mm)

☐ Lion Brand® stitch markers

☐ Lion Brand® large-eyed
blunt needle

NOTES

1. Top is made from two rectangles: one for the Back/Sleeves
   and one for the Front.

2. Each piece is worked from side to side.

3. Rectangles are folded and sewn together following a diagram.

BACK/SLEEVES

Ch 98 (102).

Row 1: Dc in 4th ch from hook (3 skipped ch count as first dc) and in each ch across – you will have 96 (100) dc.

Row 2: Ch 3 (counts as dc), turn, sk first st, dc in each st across working last dc in top of beg ch-3.

Rep Row 2 until piece measures about 45 (50) in. **[114.5 (127) cm]** from beg.

Fasten off.

FRONT

Ch 98 (102).

Row 1: Dc in 4th ch from hook (3 skipped ch count as first dc) and in each ch across – you will have 96 (100) dc.

Row 2: Ch 3 (counts as dc), turn, sk first st, dc in each st across working last dc in top of beg ch-3.

Rep Row 2 until piece measures about 21 (25) in. **[53.5 (63.5) cm]** from beg.

Fasten off.

FINISHING

Following diagrams on page 15, sew pieces together.

1. **Sew shoulder seams:** Place Back/Sleeves onto a flat surface with longer edges at top and bottom. Place markers on top edge about 17 (19) in. **[43 (48.5) cm]** from each corner, leaving center 11 (12) in. **[28 (30.5) cm]** open for neck. Place markers on one side edge of Front about 5 (6½) in. **[12.5 (16.5) cm]** from corners, leaving center 11 (12) in. **[28 (30.5) cm]** open for neck. Place Front on top of Back/Sleeves with markers matching. Sew shoulder seams between markers and Front corners.

2. **Fold Sleeves:** Place marker in center of each side edge of Front. Fold corners on each side of Back/Sleeves so that corners meet at center marker on Front side edge.

3. **Sew side seams:** Sew side edges of Front to edges of sleeves.

Weave in ends.

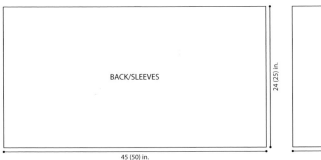

BACK/SLEEVES

24 (25) in.

45 (50) in.

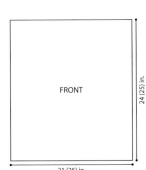

FRONT

24 (25) in.

21 (25) in.

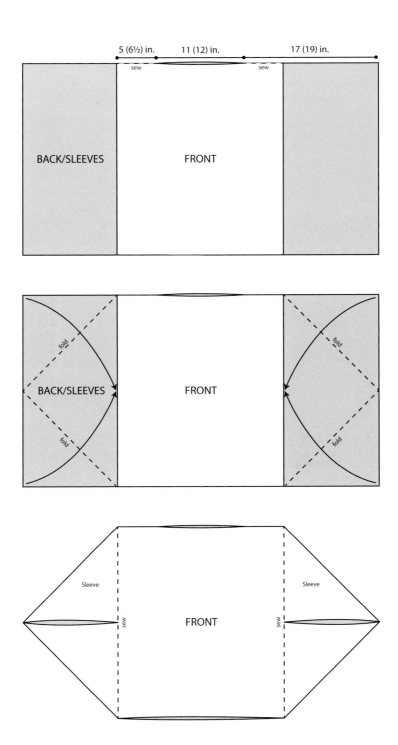

LION BRAND® COBOO

Short Hills Shell

 **EASY**

SIZES

S (M, L, 1X, 2X)

Finished Chest:
36 (40, 44, 48, 52) in.
[91.5 (101.5, 112, 122, 132) cm]

Finished Length:
21 (21½, 22, 22½, 23) in.
[53.5 (54.5, 56, 57, 58.5) cm]

Note: Pattern is written for smallest size with changes for larger sizes in parentheses. When only one number is given, it applies to all sizes. To follow pattern more easily, circle all numbers pertaining to your size before beginning.

GAUGE

29 dc = about 6 in. (15 cm);
11 rows = about 4 in. (10 cm).

BE SURE TO CHECK YOUR GAUGE.

MATERIALS

Yarn (Light) [3]
Lion Brand® COBOO
(Art. #835)

☐ #109 Steel Blue
4 (4, 5, 5, 6) balls

☐ Lion Brand® large-eyed blunt needle

Additional Materials

Crochet hook size D-3 (3.25 mm)

NOTES

1. Shell is made in 2 pieces: Back and Front.

2. Back and Front are worked back and forth in rows from lower edge upwards.

3. An edging is worked around the neck and armholes.

STITCH EXPLANATION

dc2tog (dc 2 sts together)

(Yarn over, insert hook in next st and draw up a loop, yarn over and draw through 2 loops) twice, yarn over and draw through all 3 loops on hook – 1 st decreased.

BACK

Ch 88 (98, 107, 117, 126).

Row 1 (RS): Sc in 2nd ch from hook and in each ch across – you will have 87 (97, 106, 116, 125) sc in this row.

Row 2: Ch 3 (counts as dc), turn, sk first st, dc in each st across.

Rows 3-38: Ch 3 (counts as dc), turn, sk first st, dc in each st across working last dc in top of beg ch-3.

Shape Armholes

Row 1 (RS): Ch 1, turn, sl st in first 6 (7, 8, 9, 9) sts, ch 3 (counts as dc), sk next st, dc2tog, dc in each st to last 9 (10, 11, 12, 12) sts, dc2tog, dc in next st; leave last 6 (7, 8, 9, 9) sts unworked – 73 (81, 88, 96, 105) sts.

Rows 2-5 (6, 8, 9, 10): Ch 3 (counts as dc), turn, sk first st, dc2tog, dc in each st to last 3 sts, dc2tog, dc in top of beg ch-3 – 65 (71, 74, 80, 87) dc when all decreases have been completed.

Next 9 Rows: Ch 3 (counts as dc), turn, sk first st, dc in each st across working last dc in top of beg ch-3.

First Shoulder

NOTE: For sizes S and 1X, Row 1 of first shoulder will be a RS row and this will be the right shoulder. For sizes M, L, and 2X, Row 1 of first shoulder will be a WS row and this will be the left shoulder.

Row 1: Ch 3 (counts as dc), turn, sk first st, dc in next 11 (14, 15, 17, 19) dc, dc2tog, dc in next st; leave rem sts unworked for second shoulder – 14 (17, 18, 20, 22) dc.

Row 2: Ch 3 (counts as dc), turn, sk first st, dc2tog, dc in each st across working last dc in top of beg ch-3 – 13 (16, 17, 19, 21) dc.

Row 3: Ch 3 (counts as dc), turn, sk first st, dc in each st to last 3 sts, dc2tog, dc in top of beg ch-3 – 12 (15, 16, 18, 20) dc.

Rows 4 and 5: Ch 3, turn, sk first st, dc in each st across working last dc in top of beg ch-3.

Fasten off.

Second Shoulder

NOTE: For sizes S and 1X, Row 1 of second shoulder will be a RS row and this will be the left shoulder. For sizes M, L, and 2X, Row 1 of second shoulder will be a WS row and this will be the right shoulder.

Row 1: From same side as Row 1 of first shoulder, sk the next 35 (35, 36, 38, 41) unworked sts following Row 1 of first shoulder for back neck, draw up a loop of yarn in the next st, ch 3 (counts as dc), sk same st as joining, dc2tog, dc in each st across working last st in top of beg ch-3 – 14 (17, 18, 20, 22) dc.

Row 2: Ch 3 (counts as dc), turn, sk first st, dc in each st to last 3 sts, dc2tog, dc in top of beg ch-3 – 13 (16, 17, 19, 21) dc.

Row 3: Ch 3 (counts as dc), turn, sk first st, dc2tog, dc in each st across working last dc in top of beg ch-3 – 12 (15, 16, 18, 20) dc.

Rows 4 and 5: Ch 3, turn, sk first st, dc in each st across working last dc in top of beg ch-3.

Fasten off.

FRONT

Make same as Back to Shape Armholes.

Shape Armholes

Row 1 (RS): Ch 1, turn, sl st in first 6 (7, 8, 9, 9) sts, ch 3 (counts as dc), sk next st, dc2tog, dc in each st to last 9 (10, 11, 12, 12) sts, dc2tog, dc in next st; leave last 6 (7, 8, 9, 9) sts unworked – 73 (81, 88, 96, 105) sts.

Rows 2-5 (6, 8, 9, 10): Ch 3 (counts as dc), turn, sk first st, dc2tog, dc in each st to last 3 sts, dc2tog, dc in top of beg ch-3 – 65 (71, 74, 80, 87) dc when all decreases have been completed.

Next Row: Ch 3 (counts as dc), turn, sk first st, dc in each st across working last dc in top of beg ch-3.

First Shoulder

NOTE: For sizes S and 1X, Row 1 of first shoulder will be a RS row and this will be the left shoulder. For sizes M, L, and 2X, Row 1 of first shoulder will be a WS row and this will be the right shoulder.

Row 1: Ch 3 (counts as dc), turn, sk first st, dc in next 19 (22, 23, 25, 27) dc, dc2tog, dc in next st; leave rem sts unworked for second shoulder – 22 (25, 26, 28, 30) dc.

Row 2: Ch 3 (counts as dc), turn, sk first st, (dc2tog) twice, dc in each st across working last dc in top of beg ch-3 – 20 (23, 24, 26, 28) dc.

Row 3: Ch 3 (counts as dc), turn, sk first st, dc in each st to last 3 sts, dc2tog, dc in top of beg ch-3 – 19 (22, 23, 25, 27) dc.

Rows 4-7: Rep Rows 2 and 3 twice – 13 (16, 17, 19, 21) dc.

Row 8: Ch 3 (counts as dc), turn, sk first st, dc2tog, dc in each st across working last dc in top of beg ch-3 – 12 (15, 16, 18, 20) dc.

Next 5 Rows: Ch 3 (counts as dc), turn, dc in each st across working last dc in top of beg ch-3.

Fasten off.

Second Shoulder

NOTE: For sizes S and 1X, Row 1 of second shoulder will be a RS row and this will be the right shoulder. For sizes M, L, and 2X, Row 1 of second shoulder will be a WS row and this will be the left shoulder.

Row 1: From same side as Row 1 of first shoulder, sk the next 19 (19, 20, 22, 25) unworked sts following Row 1 of first shoulder for front neck, draw up a loop of yarn in the next st, ch 3 (counts as dc), sk same st as joining, dc2tog, dc in each st across working last st in top of beg ch-3 – 22 (25, 26, 28, 30) dc.

Row 2: Ch 3 (counts as dc), turn, sk first st, dc in each st to last 3 sts, (dc2tog) twice, dc in top of beg ch-3 – 20 (23, 24, 26, 28) dc.

Row 3: Ch 3 (counts as dc), turn, sk first st, dc2tog, dc in each st across working last st in top of beg ch-3 – 19 (22, 23, 25, 27) dc.

Rows 4-7: Rep Rows 2 and 3 twice – 13 (16, 17, 19, 21) dc.

Row 8: Ch 3 (counts as dc), turn, sk first st, dc in each st across to last 3 sts, dc2tog, dc in top of beg ch-3 – 12 (15, 16, 18, 20) dc.

Next 5 Rows: Ch 3 (counts as dc), turn, dc in each st across working last dc in top of beg ch-3.

Fasten off.

FINISHING

Sew shoulder and side seams.

Armhole Edging

Rnd 1 (RS): From RS, join yarn with a sl st in one underarm, ch 1, sc evenly spaced around armhole edge; join with sl st in first sc.

Rnd 2 (RS): Ch 1, sc in each st around; join with sl st in first sc.

Fasten off.

Repeat edging around second armhole.

Neck Edging

From RS, join yarn with a sl st in either shoulder seam. Work edging same as armhole edging around neck.

Fasten off.

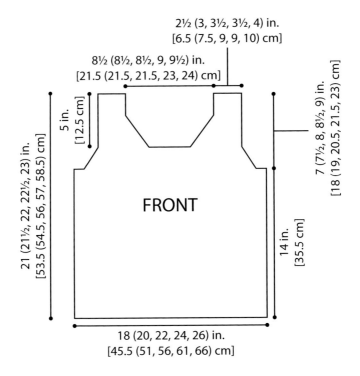

2½ (3, 3½, 3½, 4) in.
[6.5 (7.5, 9, 9, 10) cm]

8½ (8½, 8½, 9, 9½) in.
[21.5 (21.5, 21.5, 23, 24) cm]

5 in.
[12.5 cm]

7 (7½, 8, 8½, 9) in.
[18 (19, 20.5, 21.5, 23) cm]

21 (21½, 22, 22½, 23) in.
[53.5 (54.5, 56, 57, 58.5) cm]

FRONT

14 in.
[35.5 cm]

18 (20, 22, 24, 26) in.
[45.5 (51, 56, 61, 66) cm]

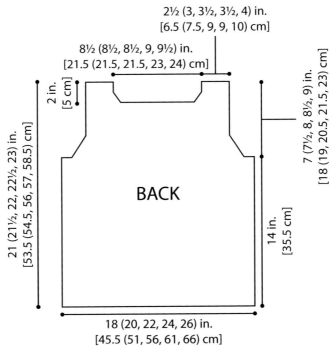

2½ (3, 3½, 3½, 4) in.
[6.5 (7.5, 9, 9, 10) cm]

8½ (8½, 8½, 9, 9½) in.
[21.5 (21.5, 21.5, 23, 24) cm]

2 in.
[5 cm]

7 (7½, 8, 8½, 9) in.
[18 (19, 20.5, 21.5, 23) cm]

21 (21½, 22, 22½, 23) in.
[53.5 (54.5, 56, 57, 58.5) cm]

BACK

14 in.
[35.5 cm]

18 (20, 22, 24, 26) in.
[45.5 (51, 56, 61, 66) cm]

LION BRAND® CUPCAKE®

Cotswold Ripple Afghan

■■□□▷ **EASY**

SIZES

About 42 x 52 in.
(106.5 x 132 cm)

GAUGE

1 ripple = about 3½ in. (9 cm)
measured from peak to peak.

BE SURE TO CHECK YOUR GAUGE.

MATERIALS

Yarn (Light)

Lion Brand® CUPCAKE®
(Art. #935)

☐ #213 Sea Breeze 1 cake (A)

☐ #201 Pot of Gold 1 cake (B)

☐ #223 Apple Picking 1 cake (C)

☐ #202 Robin Egg 1 cake (D)

☐ Lion Brand® crochet hook
size H-8 (5 mm)

☐ Lion Brand® large-eyed
blunt needle

NOTES

1. Afghan is worked in one piece in a ripple crochet pattern. The ripple pattern is easy to do, but it's important to remember that you may need to work several rows before the ripple pattern becomes clear.

2. After Row 2, 3-dc groups and clusters are worked into sps between sts, instead of in top of sts. The ripples are created by skipping 2 clusters to form 'valleys' and working (3 dc, ch 3, 3 dc) to form 'peaks'. In each row, take care to skip the 2 clusters in each 'valley' and work (3 dc, ch 3, 3 dc) in ch-3 sp at each 'peak.'

3. Yarn color is changed following a Stripe Sequence. To change yarn color, work last st of old color to last yarn over. Yarn over with new color and draw through all loops on hook to complete st. Proceed with new color. Fasten off old color.

4. For those who find a visual helpful, we've included a stitch diagram.

STITCH EXPLANATION

3-dc Cl (3 double crochet cluster)
Yarn over, insert hook in indicated st, yarn over and draw up a loop, yarn over and draw through 2 loops on hook (2 loops rem on hook), (yarn over, insert hook in same st, yarn over and draw up a loop, yarn over and draw through 2 loops on hook) twice; yarn over and draw through all 4 loops on hook.

STRIPE SEQUENCE

Work first 21 rows with A, then work 20 rows each with B and C. Work last 21 rows with D.

AFGHAN

With A, ch 207.

Row 1: Sc in 2nd ch from hook and in each ch across – you will have 206 sc in this row.

Row 2: Ch 3 (counts as first dc), turn, sk first 3 sts, (3 dc in next st, sk next 2 sts) twice, (3 dc, ch 3, 3 dc) in next st, *sk next 2 sts, 3 dc in next st, sk next 2 sts, 3-dc Cl in next st, sk next 4 sts, 3-dc Cl in next st, sk next 2 sts, 3 dc in next st, sk next 2 sts, (3 dc, ch 3, 3 dc) in next st; rep from * to last 9 sts, (sk next 2 sts, 3 dc in next st) twice, sk next 2 sts, dc in last st – 12 ripples.

Row 3: Ch 3 (counts as first dc), turn, sk next 3-dc group, (3 dc in next sp between 3-dc groups) twice, *(3 dc, ch 3, 3 dc) in next ch-3 sp, 3 dc in next sp between 3-dc groups, 3-dc Cl in next sp between 3-dc group and cluster, sk next sp between clusters, 3-dc Cl in next sp between cluster and 3-dc group, 3 dc in next sp between 3-dc groups; rep from * to last ch-3

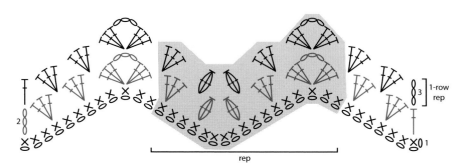

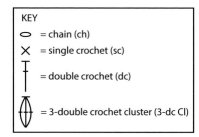

KEY

◯ = chain (ch)

✕ = single crochet (sc)

╤ = double crochet (dc)

⬥ = 3-double crochet cluster (3-dc Cl)

24

sp, (3 dc, ch 3, 3 dc) in last ch-3 sp, (3 dc in next sp between 3-dc groups) twice, dc in top of beg ch.

Rows 4-81: Rep Row 3 and continue to change color following Stripe Sequence until 20th D-colored row is completed.

Row 82: With D, ch 1, sc in each dc and 3 sc in each ch-3 sp across.

Fasten off.

FINISHING

Weave in ends.

Kenai Cowl

 **EASY**

SIZES

Finished Circumference:
About 31 in. (78.5 cm)

Finished Height:
About 14 in. (35.5 cm)

GAUGE

7 hdc + 5½ rows = about 4 in. (10 cm).

BE SURE TO CHECK YOUR GAUGE.

MATERIALS

Yarn (Super Bulky) **6** SUPER BULKY
LION BRAND® MANDALA®
THICK & QUICK® (Art. #528)

☐ #215 Garden Maze 1 cake (A)

☐ #213 Tidal 1 cake (B)

☐ Lion Brand® crochet hook size N (10 mm)

☐ Lion Brand® large-eyed blunt needle

NOTES

1. The Cowl is worked in one piece and then seamed.

2. The Cowl is worked in two colors of yarn. Yarn color A is used first, then changed to B when almost all of A has been used.

3. To change yarn color, work last st of old color to last yarn over. Yarn over with new color and draw through all loops on hook to complete st. Proceed with new color.

4. For those who find a visual helpful, we've included a stitch diagram.

COWL

With A, ch 55.

Row 1: Hdc in 3rd ch from hook (2 skipped ch count as hdc) and in each ch across – you will have 54 hdc in this row.

Row 2: Ch 3 (counts as hdc, ch 1), turn, working in back loops only, sk first 2 sts, hdc in next st, *ch 1, sk next st, hdc in next st; rep from * across, hdc in top of beg ch-2 – 28 hdc and 26 ch-1 sps.

Row 3: Ch 2 (counts as hdc), turn, 2 hdc in each ch-1 sp across, hdc in 2nd ch of beg ch-3 – 54 hdc.

NOTE: When almost all of yarn color A has been used, and ending with a Row 3 as the last row you work, change to yarn color B.

Rows 4-19: Rep Rows 2 and 3 for 8 more times.

Fasten off.

FINISHING

Sew short ends of rectangle together for about 7 in. (18 cm), leaving remaining 7 in. (18 cm) open, to make Cowl.

Weave in ends.

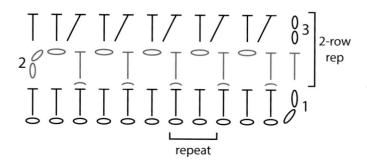

repeat

KEY

◯ = chain (ch)

T = half double crochet (hdc)

⌒ = work in back loop only

Flair Circle Vest

 **EASY+**

ONE SIZE

About 39 in. (99 cm) diameter

GAUGE

Rnds 1-8 = about 7½ in. (19 cm).

BE SURE TO CHECK YOUR GAUGE.

MATERIALS

Yarn (Light) **3**
LION BRAND® CUPCAKE®
(Art. #935)

☐ #206 Forest Path 1 cake (A)

☐ #222 Tundra 1 cake (B)

☐ Lion Brand® crochet hook
size F-5 (3.75 mm)

☐ Lion Brand® large-eyed
blunt needle

NOTES

1. Vest is worked in one piece in joined rnds with the RS always facing.

2. To change yarn color, work last stitch of old color to last yarn over.
   Yarn over with new color and draw through all loops on hook to
   complete st. Proceed with new color.

3. For those who find a visual helpful, we've included a stitch diagram
   of the first 5 rnds to help you get started.

VEST

With A, ch 6; join with sl st in first ch to form a ring.

Rnd 1 (RS): Ch 5 (counts as dc, ch 2), dc in ring, (ch 2, dc in ring) 6 times, ch 2; join with sl st in 3rd ch of beg ch-5 – you will have 8 dc and 8 ch-2 sps in this rnd.

Rnd 2: Sl st in first ch-2 sp, ch 3 (counts as dc), 2 dc in same ch-2 sp, *ch 2, 3 dc in next ch-2 sp; rep from * 6 more times, ch 2; join with sl st in top of beg ch-3 – Eight 3-dc groups and 8 ch-2 sps.

Rnd 3: Ch 3 (counts as dc), dc in same st as join, dc in next dc, 2 dc in next dc, *ch 2, sk next ch-2 sp, 2 dc in next dc, dc in next dc, 2 dc in next dc; rep from * to last ch-2 sp, ch 2, sk last ch-2 sp; join with sl st in top of beg ch-3 – Eight 5-dc groups and 8 ch-2 sps.

Rnd 4: Ch 3 (counts as dc), dc in same st as join, dc in each dc to last dc of first dc-group, 2 dc in last dc of dc-group, *ch 3, sk next ch-2 sp, 2 dc in first dc of next dc-group, dc in each dc to last dc of dc-group, 2 dc in last dc of dc-group; rep from * to last ch-2 sp, ch 3, sk last ch-2 sp; join with sl st in top of beg ch-3 – Eight 7-dc groups and 8 ch-3 sps.

....

NOTE: Continue to work with A until all of A has been used then change to B and work with B until piece is complete.

....

Rnds 5-8: Ch 3 (counts as dc), dc in same st as join, dc in each dc to last dc of first dc-group, 2 dc in last dc of dc-group, *ch 3, sk next ch-3 sp, 2 dc in first dc of next dc-group, dc in each dc to last dc of dc-group, 2 dc in last dc of dc-group; rep from * to last ch-3 sp, ch 3, sk last ch-3 sp; join with sl st in top of beg ch-3 – Eight 15-dc groups and 8 ch-3 sps in Rnd 8.

Rnd 9: Ch 3 (counts as dc), dc in same st as join, dc in each dc to last dc of first dc-group, 2 dc in last dc of dc-group, *ch 4, sk next ch-3 sp, 2 dc in first dc of next dc-group, dc in each dc to last dc of dc-group, 2 dc in last dc of dc-group; rep from * to last ch-3 sp, ch 4, sk last ch-3 sp; join with sl st in top of beg ch-3 – Eight 17-dc groups and 8 ch-4 sps.

Rnds 10-18: Ch 3 (counts as dc), dc in same st as join, dc in each dc to last dc of first dc-group, 2 dc in last dc of dc-group, *ch 4, sk next ch-4 sp, 2 dc in first dc of next dc-group, dc in each dc to last dc of dc-group, 2 dc in last dc of dc-group; rep from * to last ch-4 sp, ch 4, sk last ch-4 sp; join with sl st in top of beg ch-3 – Eight 35-dc groups and 8 ch-4 sps in Rnd 18.

Rnd 19: Ch 3 (counts as dc), dc in same st as join, dc in each dc to last dc of first dc-group, 2 dc in last dc of dc-group, ch 47 (for armhole chain), sk next ch-4 sp, sk next 35-dc groups, sk next ch-4 sp, 2 dc in first dc of next dc-group, dc in each dc to last dc of dc-group, 2 dc in last dc of dc-group, *ch 5, sk next ch-4 sp, 2 dc in first dc of next dc-group, dc in each dc to last dc of dc-group, 2 dc in last dc of dc-group; rep from * 2 more times, ch 47 (for armhole chain), sk next ch-4 sp, sk next 35-dc groups, sk next ch-4 sp, 2 dc in first dc of next dc-group, dc in each dc to last dc of dc-group, 2 dc in last dc of dc-group, ch 5, sk last ch-4 sp; join with sl st in top of beg ch-3 – Six 37-dc groups, 4 ch-5 sps, and 2 ch-47 armhole chains.

Rnd 20: Ch 3 (counts as dc), dc in same st as join, dc in each dc to last dc of first dc-group, 2 dc in last dc of dc-group; working over first armhole chain: dc in each of next 5 ch, 2 dc in next ch, dc in each of next 35 ch, 2 dc in next ch, dc in each of last 5 ch; 2 dc in first dc of next dc-group, dc in each dc to last dc of dc-group, 2 dc in last dc of dc-group, *dc in each of next 5 ch, 2 dc in first dc of next dc-group, dc in each dc to last dc of dc-group, 2 dc in last dc of dc-group; rep from * to second armhole chain; working over second armhole chain: dc in each of next 5 ch, 2 dc in next ch, dc in each of next 35 ch, 2 dc in next ch, dc in each of last 5 ch, 2 dc in first dc of next dc-group, dc in each dc to last dc of dc-group, 2 dc in last dc of dc-group, dc in each of last 5 ch; join with sl st in top of beg ch-3 – 352 dc.

Rnd 21: Ch 3 (counts as dc), dc in same st as join, dc in next 37 dc, 2 dc in next dc, *dc in next 5 dc, 2 dc in next dc, dc in next 37 dc, 2 dc in next dc; repeat from * 6 more times, dc in last 5 dc; join with sl st in top of beg ch-3 – 368 dc.

Rnd 22: Ch 3 (counts as dc), dc in same st as join, dc in next 39 dc, 2 dc in next dc, *dc in next 5 dc, 2 dc in next dc, dc in next 39 dc, 2 dc in next dc; repeat from * 6 more times, dc in last 5 dc; join with sl st in top of beg ch-3 – 384 dc.

Rnd 23: Ch 3 (counts as dc), dc in same st as join, dc in next 41 dc, 2 dc in next dc, *dc in next 5 dc, 2 dc in next dc, dc in next 41 dc, 2 dc in next dc; repeat from * 6 more times, dc in last 5 dc; join with sl st in top of beg ch-3 – 400 dc.

Rnd 24: Ch 3 (counts as dc), dc in same st as join, dc in next 43 dc, 2 dc in next dc, *dc in next 5 dc, 2 dc in next dc, dc in next 43 dc, 2 dc in next dc; repeat from * 6 more times, dc in last 5 dc; join with sl st in top of beg ch-3 – 416 dc.

Rnd 25: Ch 3 (counts as dc), dc in same st as join, dc in next 45 dc, 2 dc in next dc, *dc in next 5 dc, 2 dc in next dc, dc in next 45 dc, 2 dc in next dc; repeat from * 6 more times, dc in last 5 dc; join with sl st in top of beg ch-3 – 432 dc.

Rnd 26: Ch 3 (counts as dc), dc in same st as join, dc in next 47 dc, 2 dc in next dc, *dc in next 5 dc, 2 dc in next dc, dc in next 47 dc, 2 dc in next dc; repeat from * 6 more times, dc in last 5 dc; join with sl st in top of beg ch-3 – 448 dc.

Rnd 27: Ch 3 (counts as dc), dc in same st as join, dc in next 49 dc, 2 dc in next dc, *dc in next 5 dc, 2 dc in next dc, dc in next 49 dc, 2 dc in next dc; repeat from * 6 more times, dc in last 5 dc; join with sl st in top of beg ch-3 – 464 dc.

Rnd 28: Ch 6 (counts as dc, ch 3), sk next dc, dc in next dc, *ch 3, sk next 2 dc, dc in next dc; rep from * to last 2 dc, ch 3, sk last 2 dc; join with sl st in 3rd ch of beg ch-6 – 155 dc and 155 ch-3 sps.

Rnd 29: Ch 1, sc in same ch as join, *ch 3, sk next ch-3 sp, sc in next dc; rep from * to last ch-3 sp, ch 3, sk last ch-3 sp; join with sl st in first sc – 155 sc and 155 ch-3 sps.

Rnd 30: Ch 1, sc in same sc as join, *ch 3, sk next ch-3 sp, sc in next sc; rep from * to last ch-3 sp, ch 3, sk last ch-3 sp; join with sl st in first sc.

Rnd 31: Sl st in first ch-3 sp, ch 7 (counts as dc, ch 4), dc in next ch-3 sp, *ch 4, dc in next ch-3 sp; rep from * around, ch 4; join with sl st in 3rd ch of beg ch-7 – 155 dc and 155 ch-4 sps.

Rnd 32: Ch 1, sc in same ch as join, *ch 4, sk next ch-4 sp, sc in next dc; rep from * to last ch-4 sp, ch 4, sk last ch-4 sp; join with sl st in first sc – 155 sc and 155 ch-4 sps.

Rnd 33: Ch 1, sc in same sc as join, *ch 4, sk next ch-4 sp, sc in next sc; rep from * to last ch-4 sp, ch 4, sk last ch-4 sp; join with sl st in first sc.

Rnds 34-36: Rep Rnds 31-33.

Rnd 37: Sl st in first ch-sp, ch 8 (counts as dc, ch 5), dc in next ch-sp, *ch 5, dc in next ch-sp; rep from * around, ch 5; join with sl st in 3rd ch of beg ch-8 – 155 dc and 155 ch-5 sps.

Rnd 38: Ch 1, sc in same ch as join, *ch 5, sk next ch-5 sp, sc in next dc; rep from * to last ch-5 sp, ch 5, sk last ch-5 sp; join with sl st in first sc – 155 sc and 155 ch-5 sps.

Rnd 39: Ch 1, sc in same sc as join, *ch 5, sk next ch-5 sp, sc in next sc; rep from * to last ch-5 sp, ch 5, sk last ch-5 sp; join with sl st in first sc.

Rnds 40-45: Rep Rnds 37-39 twice.

Rnd 46: Sl st in first 3 ch of first ch-5 sp, *ch 5, sl st in next ch-5 sp; rep from * around, ch 5; join with sl st in center of first ch-5 sp.

Fasten off.

FINISHING
Weave in ends.

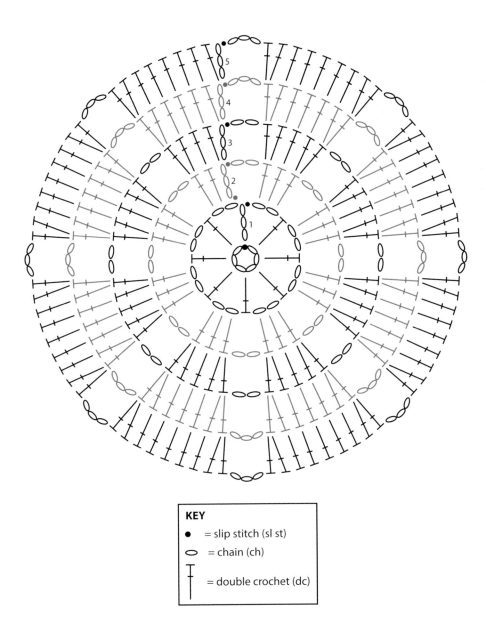

KEY

●	= slip stitch (sl st)
⬭	= chain (ch)
⊤	= double crochet (dc)

Diagonal Eyelets Shawl

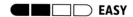 **EASY**

SIZE

About 11 x 74 in. (28 x 188 cm)

GAUGE

23 sts = about 4 in. (10 cm) over Rows 2-19 of pattern.

Notes: Each dc and ch-1 sp count as 1 st. Each ch-2 sp counts as 2 sts.

BE SURE TO CHECK YOUR GAUGE.

MATERIALS

Yarn (Lace)
LION BRAND® AMAZING LACE (Art. #213)

☐ #144 Medallion Magenta 1 cake

☐ LION BRAND® crochet hook size E-4 (3.5 mm)

☐ LION BRAND® large-eyed blunt needle

NOTES

1. Shawl is worked in one piece.
2. Follow written instructions, or read the chart, as desired. Read odd-numbered rows of chart from right to left and even-numbered rows from left to right.

SHAWL

Ch 67.

Row 1: Dc in 4th ch from hook (3 skipped ch count as dc), dc in next 3 ch, *ch 2, sk next 2 ch, dc in next 7 ch; rep from * to last 6 ch, ch 2, sk next 2 ch, dc in last 4 ch – you will have 7 ch-2 sps and 8 dc-groups (one 5-dc group at beg of row, one 4-dc group at end of row, and six 7-dc groups) in this row.

Row 2: Ch 3 (counts as dc), turn, sk first st, dc in next dc, *ch 2, sk next 2 dc, 2 dc in next ch-2 sp, dc in next 5 dc; rep from * across working last dc in top of beg ch-3 – 7 ch-2 sps and 8 dc-groups (one 2-dc group at beg of row and seven 7-dc groups).

Row 3: Ch 4 (counts as dc, ch 1), turn, sk first 2 sts, dc in next 5 dc, 2 dc in next ch-2 sp, *ch 2, sk next 2 dc, dc in next 5 dc, 2 dc in next ch-2 sp; rep from * 5 more times, ch 1, sk next dc, dc in top of beg ch-3 – 2 ch-1 sps, 6 ch-2 sps, 1 dc at beg and end of row, and seven 7-dc groups.

Row 4: Ch 3 (counts as dc), turn, sk first st, dc in first ch-1 sp, dc in next 5 dc, *ch 2, sk next 2 dc, 2 dc in next ch-2 sp, dc in next 5 dc; rep from * 5 more times, ch 2, sk next 2 dc, dc in beg ch-sp, dc in 3rd ch of beg ch-4 – 7 ch-2 sps, one 2-dc group at end of row, and seven 7-dc groups.

Row 5: Ch 3 (counts as dc), turn, sk first st, dc in next dc, 2 dc in next ch-2 sp, *ch 2, sk next 2 dc, dc in next 5 dc, 2 dc in next ch-2 sp; rep from * 5 more times, ch 2, sk next 2 dc, dc in next 4 dc, dc in top of beg ch-3 – 7 ch-2 sps, one 4-dc group at beg of row, one 5-dc group at end of row, and six 7-dc groups.

Row 6: Ch 3 (counts as dc), turn, sk first st, dc in next 2 dc, *ch 2, sk next 2 dc, 2 dc in next ch-2 sp, dc in next 5 dc; rep from * 5 more times, ch 2, sk next 2 dc, 2 dc in next ch-2 sp, dc in next 3 dc, dc in top of beg ch-3 – 7 ch-2 sps, one 3-dc group at beg of row, one 6-dc group at end of row, and six 7-dc groups.

Row 7: Ch 3 (counts as dc), turn, sk first st, dc in next 5 dc, 2 dc in next ch-2 sp, *ch 2, sk next 2 dc, dc in next 5 dc, 2 dc in next ch-2 sp; rep from * 5 more times, ch 2, sk next 2 dc, dc in top of beg ch-3 – 7 ch-2 sps, one 8-dc group at beg of row, 1 dc at end of row, and six 7-dc groups.

Row 8: Ch 3 (counts as dc), turn, sk first st, 2 dc in first ch-2 sp, dc in next 5 dc, *ch 2, sk next 2 dc, 2 dc in next ch-2 sp, dc in next 5 dc; rep from * 5 more times, ch 2, sk next 2 dc, dc in top of beg ch-3 – 7 ch-2 sps, one 8-dc group at beg of row, 1 dc at end of row, and six 7-dc groups.

Row 9: Ch 3 (counts as dc), turn, sk first dc, *2 dc in next ch-2 sp, ch 2, sk next 2 dc, dc in next 5 dc; rep from * to beg ch, dc in top of beg ch-3 – 7 ch-2 sps, one 3-dc group at beg of row, one 6-dc group at end of row, and six 7-dc groups.

Row 10: Ch 3 (counts as dc), turn, sk first st, dc in next 3 dc, *ch 2, sk next 2 dc, 2 dc in next ch-2 sp, dc in next 5 dc; rep from * 5 more times, ch 2, sk next 2 dc, 2 dc in next ch-2 sp, dc in next 2 dc, dc in top of beg ch-3 – 7 ch-2 sps, one 4-dc group at beg of row, one 5-dc group at end of row, and six 7-dc groups.

Row 11: Ch 3 (counts as dc), turn, sk first st, dc in next 4 dc, 2 dc in next ch-2 sp, *ch 2, sk next 2 dc, dc in next 5 dc, 2 dc in next ch-2 sp; rep from * 5 more times, ch 2, sk next 2 dc, dc in next dc, dc in top of beg ch-3 – 7 ch-2 sps, one 2-dc group at end of row, and seven 7-dc groups.

Row 12: Ch 4 (counts as dc, ch 1), turn, sk first 2 sts, 2 dc in next ch-2 sp, *dc in next 5 dc, ch 2, sk next 2 dc, 2 dc in next ch-2 sp; rep from * 5 more times, dc in next 5 dc, ch 1, sk next dc, dc in top of beg ch-3 – 2 ch-1 sps, 6 ch-2 sps, 1 dc at beg and end of row, and seven 7-dc groups.

Row 13: Ch 3 (counts as dc), turn, sk first st, dc in first ch-1 sp, *ch 2, sk next 2 dc, dc in next 5 dc, 2 dc in next ch-2 sp; rep from * 5 more times, ch 2, sk next 2 dc, dc in next 5 dc, dc in beg ch-sp, dc in 3rd ch of beg ch-4 – 7 ch-2 sps, one 2-dc group at beg of row, and seven 7-dc groups.

Row 14: Ch 3 (counts as dc), turn, sk first st, dc in next 4 dc, *ch 2, sk next 2 dc, 2 dc in next ch-2 sp, dc in next 5 dc; rep from * 5 more times, ch 2, sk next 2 dc, 2 dc in next ch-2 sp, dc in next dc, dc in top of beg ch-3 – 7 ch-2 sps, one 5-dc group at beg of row, one 4-dc group at end of row, and six 7-dc groups.

Row 15: Ch 3 (counts as dc), turn, sk first st, dc in next 3 dc, 2 dc in next ch-2 sp, *ch 2, sk next 2 dc, dc in next 5 dc, 2 dc in next ch-2 sp; rep from * 5 more times, ch 2, sk next 2 dc, dc in next 2 dc, dc in top of beg ch-3 – 7 ch-2 sps, one 6-dc group at beg of row, one 3-dc group at end of row, and six 7-dc groups.

Row 16: Ch 5 (counts as dc, ch 2), turn, sk first 3 sts, 2 dc in next ch-2 sp, dc in next 5 dc, *ch 2, sk next 2 dc, 2 dc in next ch-2 sp, dc in next 5 dc; rep from * across, dc in top of beg ch-3 – 7 ch-2 sps, 1 dc at beg of row, one 8-dc group at end of row, and six 7-dc groups.

Row 17: Ch 5 (counts as dc, ch 2), turn, sk first 3 sts, dc in next 5 dc, 2 dc in next ch-2 sp, *ch 2, sk next 2 dc, dc in next 5 dc, 2 dc in next ch-2 sp; rep from * 4 more times, ch 2, sk next 2 dc, dc in next 5 dc, 2 dc in beg ch-sp, dc in 3rd ch of beg ch-5 – 7 ch-2 sps, 1 dc at beg of row, one 8-dc group at end of row, and six 7-dc groups.

Row 18: Ch 3 (counts as dc), turn, sk first st, dc in next 5 dc, *ch 2, sk next 2 dc, 2 dc in next ch-2 sp, dc in next 5 dc; rep from * 5 more times, ch 2, sk next 2 dc, 2 dc in beg ch-sp, dc in 3rd ch of beg ch-5 – 7 ch-2 sps, one 6-dc group at beg of row, one 3-dc group at end of row, and six 7-dc groups.

Row 19: Ch 3 (counts as dc), turn, sk first st, dc in next 2 dc, 2 dc in next ch-2 sp, *ch 2, sk next 2 dc, dc in next 5 dc, 2 dc in next ch-2 sp; rep from * 5 more times, ch 2, sk next 2 dc, dc in next 3 dc, dc in top of beg ch-3 – 7 ch-2 sps, one 5-dc group at beg of row, one 4-dc group at end of row, and six 7-dc groups.

Rep Rows 2-19 until piece measures about 74 in. (188 cm) from beg.

Fasten off.

FINISHING
Weave in ends.

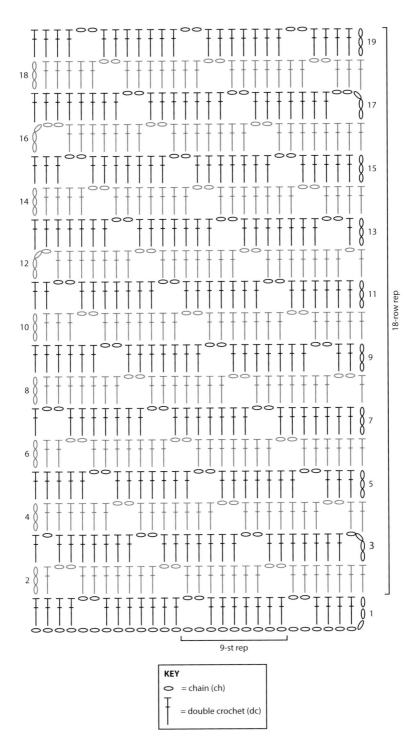

KEY

◯ = chain (ch)

𝖳 = double crochet (dc)

41

LION BRAND® MANDALA® THICK & QUICK®

Wild Weekend Afghan

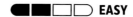 **EASY**

SIZE

About 38½ x 52 in.
(98 x 132 cm)

GAUGE

2 (3 dc, ch 1) groups = about 4 in.
(10 cm).

BE SURE TO CHECK YOUR GAUGE.

MATERIALS

Yarn (Super Bulky) **6** SUPER BULKY
Lion Brand® MANDALA®
THICK & QUICK® (Art. #528)

- ☐ #210 Pinwheel 2 cakes (A)
- ☐ #200 Labyrinth 1 cake (B)
- ☐ #201 Swirl 1 cake (C)
- ☐ #204 Vortex 1 cake (D)
- ☐ #213 Tidal 1 cake (E)
- ☐ #205 Whirl 1 cake (F)
- ☐ #202 Curlicue 1 cake (G)
- ☐ Lion Brand® crochet hook size P-15 (10 mm)
- ☐ Lion Brand® large-eyed blunt needle

NOTES

1. Afghan is worked in one piece, back and forth in rows, changing yarn color when you've used an entire cake of one color. You can change yarn colors anywhere in the row.

2. To change yarn color, work last st of old color to last yarn over. Yarn over with new color and draw through all loops to complete st. Proceed with new color. Fasten off old color.

AFGHAN

With A, ch 79.

Row 1: With A, 3 dc in 7th ch from hook (6 skipped ch count as base ch, dc, ch 1), *ch 1, sk next 3 ch, 3 dc in next ch; rep from * to last 4 ch, ch 1, sk next 3 ch, dc in last ch – Eighteen 3-dc groups.

Row 2: Ch 3 (counts as dc), turn, 2 dc in first ch-1 sp, *ch 1, sk next 3 dc, 3 dc in next ch-1 sp; rep from * to last 3-dc group, ch 1, sk next 3 dc, 3 dc in beg ch-sp – Nineteen 3-dc groups.

Row 3: Ch 4 (counts as dc, ch 1), turn, sk first 3 dc, 3 dc in next ch-1 sp, *ch 1, sk next 3 dc, 3 dc in next ch-1 sp; rep from * to last 3 dc, ch 1, sk next 2 dc, dc in top of beg ch-3.

With A, rep Rows 2 and 3 until almost all of one cake of A has been used.

You will now be simply repeating Rows 2 and 3, changing yarn color each time you finish one cake of yarn.

Change yarn color as follows:

Use all of each cake of B, C, D, E, F and G.

Change to the second cake of A, and continue to repeat Rows 2 and 3 until you haven't enough yarn to complete another row.

Fasten off.

FINISHING

Weave in ends.

General Instructions

ABBREVIATIONS

beg	begin(ning)
ch(s)	chain(s)
ch-sp(s)	chain space(s) previously made
Cl	Cluster
cm	centimeters
dc	double crochet(s)
dc2tog	double crochet 2 together
hdc	half double crochet(s)
mm	millimeters
RS	right side
rem	remain(ing)
rep	repeat
Rnd(s)	round(s)
sc	single crochet(s)
sk	skip
sl st	slip stitch
sp(s)	space(s)
st(s)	stitch(es)
WS	wrong side

CROCHET TERMINOLOGY

UNITED STATES		INTERNATIONAL
slip stitch (slip st)	=	single crochet (sc)
single crochet (sc)	=	double crochet (dc)
half double crochet (hdc)	=	half treble crochet (htr)
double crochet (dc)	=	treble crochet (tr)
treble crochet (tr)	=	double treble crochet (dtr)
double treble crochet (dtr)	=	triple treble crochet (ttr)
triple treble crochet (tr tr)	=	quadruple treble crochet (qtr)
skip	=	miss

CROCHET HOOKS

U.S.	Metric mm
B-1	2.25
C-2	2.75
D-3	3.25
E-4	3.5
F-5	3.75
G-6	4
7	4.5
H-8	5
I-9	5.5
J-10	6
K-10½	6.5
L-11	8
M/N-13	9
N/P-15	10
P/Q	15
Q	16
S	19

●□□□ **BASIC**	Projects using basic stitches. May include basic increases and decreases.	
●■□□ **EASY**	Projects may include simple stitch patterns, color work, and/or shaping.	
●■■□ **INTERMEDIATE**	Projects may include involved stitch patterns, color work, and/or shaping.	
●■■■ **COMPLEX**	Projects may include complex stitch patterns, color work, and/or shaping using a variety of techniques and stitches simultaneously.	

Yarn Weight Symbol & Names	LACE (0)	SUPER FINE (1)	FINE (2)	LIGHT (3)	MEDIUM (4)	BULKY (5)	SUPER BULKY (6)	JUMBO (7)
Type of Yarns in Category	Fingering, size 10 crochet thread	Sock, Fingering, Baby	Sport, Baby	DK, Light Worsted	Worsted, Afghan, Aran	Chunky, Craft, Rug	Super Bulky, Roving	Jumbo, Roving
Crochet Gauge* Ranges in Single Crochet to 4" (10 cm)	32-42 sts**	21-32 sts	16-20 sts	12-17 sts	11-14 sts	8-11 sts	6-9 sts	5 sts and fewer
Advised Hook Size Range	Steel*** 6 to 8, Regular hook B-1	B-1 to E-4	E-4 to 7	7 to I-9	I-9 to K-10½	K-10½ to M/N-13	M/N-13 to Q	Q and larger

*GUIDELINES ONLY: The chart above reflects the most commonly used gauges and hook sizes for specific yarn categories.

** Lace weight yarns are usually crocheted with larger hooks to create lacy openwork patterns. Accordingly, a gauge range is difficult to determine. Always follow the gauge stated in your pattern.

SYMBOLS & TERMS

* — work instructions following * as many **more** times as indicated in addition to the first time.

** to ** — work all instructions from first ** to second ** **as many** times as specified.

( ) or [ ] — work enclosed instructions **as many** times as specified by the number immediately following **or** work all enclosed instructions in the stitch or space indicated **or** contains explanatory remarks.

GAUGE

Exact gauge is essential for proper size. Before beginning your project, make a sample swatch in the yarn and hook specified in the individual instructions. After completing the swatch, measure it, counting your stitches and rows/rounds carefully. If your swatch is larger or smaller than specified, **make another, changing hook size to get the correct gauge**. Keep trying until you find the size hook that will give you the specified gauge.

BACK LOOP ONLY

Work only in loop(s) indicated by arrow *(Fig. 1)*.

Fig. 1

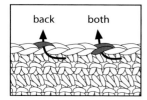

CHANGING COLORS

Work the last stitch to within one step of completion, hook new yarn *(Fig. 2a or 2b)* and draw through both loops on hook.

Fig. 2a

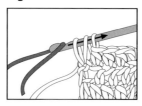

Fig. 2b

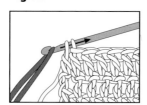

WORKING IN SPACE BEFORE A STITCH

When instructed to work in space **before** a stitch or in spaces **between** stitches, insert hook in space indicated by arrow *(Fig. 3)*.

Fig. 3

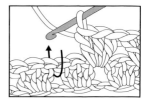